And the words you put down will be magic

Charlie Knowlton

Copyright© 2022 Charlie Knowlton
ISBN: 978-81-8253-912-9

First Edition: 2022
Rs. 200/-

Cyberwit.net
HIG 45 Kaushambi Kunj, Kalindipuram
Allahabad - 211011 (U.P.) India
http://www.cyberwit.net
Tel: +(91) 9415091004
E-mail: info@cyberwit.net

Printed at Vcore Connect LLP.

Contents

"June, precious June."

June, precious June,
prettiest girl in the room.
You're the bride
of the wedding
in lilac perfume.
The scent of a rose
a child's drink
from the hose,
a firefly sprinkle
as day comes to close.
You're the belle of the ball,
the ground robin's call,
the green leaf of maple
that knows not of Fall.
A hummingbird's visit
that vague deja vu,
morning dew on the meadow
that's gone before noon.
So June, precious June,
must you leave us so soon,
won't you stay
for the summer,
like the peony blooms?

"Date night."

Come take my hand
and let us walk for a while.
Bring your goodness, your beauty,
that strawberry blond smile.
To an open buffet
of laughter and play,
with honey dipped toppings
a cherry souffle'
Where we'll swirl and twirl
through God's given treats.
Unfurl a whirl
into heavenly sweets.
An evening of bliss
not costing a cent.
Then lie beneath
that fortune
cookie tree of content.

"Come back! We wrote you this poem."

She said she liked my poems
and asked if I would go write her one.
I explained I cannot go to them
they have to come to me.
She did not understand
and sadly walked away.
Just then a poem came to me
and asked, why is she so sad?
I said she wanted a poem
but I did not have one.
And the poem asked, why not?
And I replied,
I did not know you were coming.
And the poem said,
well I am here now
so let us write her a poem
and make her happy.
And we wrote her this poem.

"And just like that."

And just like that
one swing of the ax,
Autumn's been felled
and winter is back.
With shivering maples
the sun in reverse,
the snow laden boughs
of balsam and birch.
The streams have gone silent,
the birds without verse,
our days now in darkness,
the tilt of the earth.

"Orange is the new Autumn."

Orange is the new Autumn,
and my pumpkin spice candle.
First flicker in the stove box
stickmatch on the mantle.
Warm bisque on the burner
canning jars off the shelf,
crooked stack of split maple
unstacking itself.
Leaves whistle through the garden
past tomato stake tombs,
now a chicken wired graveyard
of yellow squash bones.
The hills now in auburn
the sky sullen gray,
soon my 70th winter,
life is good
think i'll stay.

"A moment in chime."

The little legs
of my wind chimes dangle
and giggle a nervous tune,
each time a soft breeze
tickles the soles
of their feet.
And as a blue bird
on a red tin roof
looks on with indifference,
for a moment
I am 8 years old again.
A time when time itself
did not move.
And everything,
a simple
and joyous
wonder.

"Fort Dix N.J. August, 1971."

They took away
my peacenik beads
and things
I like to puff.
My bell bottom
worn out jeans,
blue, with paisley cuffs.
Dressed head to toe
in olive drab and
taught me how to march,
shaved my head,
learned ways to kill,
2 years without
my fluff.

"Lilacs in May."

Like taking
the prettiest girl,
in a purple lace gown,
to the fragrance ball.

"The power of lilacs."

If nations gathered
when the lilac blooms.
That colorful cluster
of fragrant plume.
then peace be born
from loving womb,
and save young men
from senseless tomb.

"Michelle`s cat Smiddy."

Michelle's cat Smiddy,
is 19 years old.
When I pick him up,
his fur comes off.
When I put him down,
his fur comes off.
Michelle says,
she would like him
to sleep with us.
I say, I would
like a divorce.
Michelle says,
but we're not married.
I say, oh!
I guess i'll
go walk Lucy.
She's my dog.

"Breakfast with Lucy."

my yellow lab.

Wisping kitchen sunlight
through dust and wood smoke.
Golden hairs from her body
with a shake as she woke.
Rising up gently
softly down as they float.
And brushing my oatmeal
with a fresh yellow coat.

"And the words you put down will be magic."

Hang tough little ones.
Hang tough as you walk
through the
gauntlet of scorn
and fists of the bully.
Hang tough and you will
come out the other side.
And when you do
you will feel and think
more deeply
and see things
that others cannot.
And when you think, and feel,
and see more deeply,
your hearts will beat music,
your brush will splash rainbows,
and the words you put down
will be magic.

"Spring poem of unity."

Yellow bugled daffodils
that trumpet in the Spring.
The tulip and the crocus,
and the hopeful hearts
they bring.
Let April melt the icy chill
of hatred that we spill.
Thawing out our differences,
one people we are still.

"Sweet signs of Spring."

From window to window
chasing early March sun.
A calico kitten
in the red geraniums.
And peeks through
torn plastic that flips
in the breeze.
To a creamsicle daybreak
oer the rock maple trees.
A thaw stirs the crocus
and it's freeze, melt freeze,
5 below zero
now it's 50 degrees.
The streams break and flow
as mud hits the road,
all sweet signs
of springtime,
like sugar on snow.

"Tequila sunrise."

If one were to look east,
through the wrong
end of binoculars
on this clear and cold
early January morning,
they just may see
a lit match
riding an icecube
to Denver.
Or perhaps just
a smaller version
of daybreak.
For today the sun rose
like a slice of lemon
that grips the salty edge
of an ice cold margarita
badly in need of
another shot of tequila
for warmth.

" Your very best."

Sometimes a poem
just comes to you,
like a loyal pet
when called.
Written in
a moments time
when chaotic thought
has stalled.
A time when all
emotions peak
yet mind remains
sedated,
you hit the ball
right out
of the park,
touching home with
what's created.

"Obituary of a moth."

You arrived early Spring,
on white powdered wings
to the heat of a bulb
if touched it would sting.
You bobbed and you weaved
while taking your dings,
like a staggering drunk
or fighter in the ring.
Then a ZAP! and a FLASH!
you fell to the ground.
Moth was knocked out
for good, in the
13th round.

Moth...May 3, 2017 - May 5, 2017.

Was hatched, grew wings,
headed to the nearest lightbulb
and died...
Was a life long member of
The Knights of Columbus.

"Children`s book writer's block."

Foods that begin
with the letter P
make me poop.
Peaches, pears, plums,
...pineapples........
pananas?.....Hmmm!

"Born in November."

Brown and gray
dead leaves all astray,
stalks wither in mourning
pumpkins slayed.
Dark at 5,
little time to play,
clocks retreat,
set back to save.
A gift wrapped football?
Surprise!...Again?
What's that make Mom,
9 or 10?
Just eat your cake
and when you're through,
homework, bed,
tomorrow there's school.
Birthdays in Autumn,
of which i'm a member,
65 in a row now,
all in November.

"Beauty...1959-1970."

All I remember
is she was all white
with a black ring
around one eye.
Like a mole
on the the face
of a beauty queen.
She was the
Marilyn Monroe
of dogs,
and we named
her Beauty.

"Hearts like an egg."

Hearts like an egg
forever hard boiled.
Friends that betrayed
and dreams that were foiled.
Protecting it's shell
and those whom were loyal,
toys of their youth, their health all now spoiled.
Hearts like an egg
forever hard boiled.
Decisions, regrets,
a life of turmoil.
Choices, bad bets,
and days of hard toil,
they fall to their beds,
body in coil.
Hearts like an egg
forever hard boiled.
Doing their best
only coming up roiled.
Controversial at best,
always embroiled,
and no longer fear,
going under the soil.

"The Groton forest wood crew."

"Sap melts in my hands
so sticky, icky, yicky,
like a spruce lime ricky."
Charlie! Charlie! wake up!
We accidently dropped
a tree on your head
and you started hip hoppin'
and mumbling something
about Em n Em, or M & Ms,
or maybe it was Aunty Em.
...Oh! I'm alright fellas,
I was just dreaming,
and you, and you, and you,
were all there.

"Top 10 things my dog has never said to me."

10...Can we get another cat?

9...No! As a matter of fact
we're not happy to see you.

8...That's ok!...You eat the
rest of that rib eye.

7...Do I need a mint?

6...Sorry about your friends leg,
and of course i'll pay for the pillow.

5...And where have you been?

4...Is there a 12 step group
for butt sniffing?

3...Please!...Do not rub my belly
or scratch my ears.

2...You threw it! You go get it!

And the number one thing my dog has
never said to me,
"That's your 3rd beer ya know."

The top 10 things my cat HAS said to me.

10...The dog did it.

9...It's called a bird. Where else
was I supposed to bring it?

8...Go ask the vet, it's what we do.
Sleep all day and scratch furniture.

7...Fetch?...You're kidding me right?

6...Psst!...Wanna do some nip?

5...You know what would go nice with
the love seat and sofa?
A yellow canary and some gold fish.

4...So I missed!...Maybe you should
clean it out more often.

3...Pay attention now! For the last time
it's 5 tuna, 6 chicken, 3 liver,
and a mixed seafood.

2...I could just kill
for some fresh mouse.

And the number one thing my cat
has said to me...
"Are you sure you're an Egyptian?"

"My truck is so old."

My truck is so old that when I gas up
I get a free Flinstone glass.

So old that mold, has my truck
growing on it.

So old that when I bought it used
I found Rose Kennedy's prom dress
under the seat.

My truck is so old that pot holes
cover up when they see me coming.

So old that all it's parts have
"If found" return address labels on them.

So old the seat belt's
my mothers right arm.

My truck is so old that "Mr. Sandman" is the
only song on the radio.

So old that it has a "Nixon/Agnew"
bumper sticker on it.

And finally!...My truck is so old that
when I go in for an inspection,
I have to come back the next day.
After they've stopped laughing.

"Romantic dinner gone wrong."

Was their 3rd date as the night became late.
An exciting new love, but that can wait.
With a dash of twinkle in his eye
and a spoonful of hope in her heart,
they nestled and stirred
vowing never to part.
Soft music was playing
as the red wine flowed,
mixing and blending as senses glowed.
Then it happened!...No! Not that!
The pot boiled over
nearly killing the cat.
Grabbing a cloth and removing the lid
to the shadows of the kitchen
his face became hid.
As she blew on the lid attempting to cool,
his face reappeared and she felt like a fool.
Pointing to the door he asked her to leave,
a night so special she could not believe.
Now hurt and confused and beginning to cry,
she laid down the cloth and simply asked why?
Looking down at the floor and knowing it's over,
hesitating a moment he finally told her.
I'm looking for a lover who won't blow my cover
...Take it easy!

"A brief message."

At the tone
please leave a brief message!...Beep!
Hello Bob? Are you there?
This is Charlie, and all mine have a tear.
Call me back and we'll talk underwear.
...Briefly.

"A celebrity limerick."

I don't get the Kardashian lasses.
Adored by their following masses.
Considered quite pretty
down in New york city,
who knew their was fame in fat...sunglasses.

"RSVP."

I've invited the fireflys
to come dance
with the rising embers
of my Autumn fire.
They'll get back to me,
in June.

"Spring in Northhampton."

A birds joyous flutter
in early May grand.
Bulbs pop yellow heads
from a green woken land.
Crickets and peepers
work 2nd shift chatter
as a voice out of Boston,
announces next batter.
It's springtime in Amherst,
Smith girls in light sweaters.
Where Emily penned hope,
as the thing with feathers.

"September days. A footie."

Gold haze
reap maze

Mums bloom
full moon

School bus
kids fuss

Hay fields
fruit peels

Red leaf
Fall brief

"Mid winter. A footie."

Wet feet
rain sleet

Cold breeze
cough sneeze

Dress warm
snow storm

Ear muffs
warm duff

Hot coals
soup bowls

Coat hook
good book

Soft seat
wood heat

Red pine
fine wine

One flight
nigh' night

"A kettle in the pond and some pond in the kettle."

Autumn deepens toward winter
through the eye of a crow,
the head of an owl
with a pond just below.
And a kettle in the pond
and some pond in the kettle,
and lairs in the owl
where the black bear soon settles.
And the ridge over Groton,
once amber and gold,
Lie the bones of last summer,
in November's dark hold.

"Nursery rhyme sarcasm."

Mary had a little lamb,
And a little mint jelly.

Old mother Hubbard,
died...Like I said, she was old.

I'm a little teapot,
whatever!...Just make the tea.

There was an old woman,
See old mother Hubbard...Ditto.

Little Jack Horner,
In a time out...Kid's trouble.

Humpty Dumpty sat on a wall.
Little miss Muffet sat on a tuffet.
...Seperate checks.

"Mill road, 1970, Hampden, Mass."

There were days without drink
but nary a night.
That little stone bridge
and friends getting tight.
Then acting like Moses,
they fled in a panic.
Grabbing their Buds
two stepping the Scantic.

"Craigslist Freudian slip."

Couch and 5
unneutered cats...
Free, free, free, pee, frec.

Untitled Haiku and senryu poems.

dysfunctional
family...
a bee in the car"

my missing
red sock...found
in my pink tee shirt drawer

after calling
in sick...
my normal voice

dressing in the dark...
one brown and one black shoe
...casual mondays

standing at the altar...
wearing a tuxedo
to his funeral

his dad
before the beating...
another belt of whiskey

windy day...
2 trashmen
playing frisbee

85th
class reunion...
plenty of parking

clothes dryer maintenance...
cleaning out
its belly button

now that its legal...
zig zagging
in traffic

chinese restaurant...
when no ones looking
i use the fork

handing a coke
to a polar bear...not handing
my arm back

commune living...
chicken pot
and pie dinner

veterans day...
old soldiers
popping buttons

thanksgiving...
my brother
gives me the bird

1621 the first
thanksgiving trouble maker...
im taking friday off too

retirement... my final
living expense
...more pajamas

the invisible man
hit by car...nothing to see
here folks move along

bug eyed and no place
to hide...my naked goldfish
acting koi

mad cow disease...
the cows so relieved
to be penguins

my new haiku pad...
page after page of
pre crumpled paper

how quickly
time passes...this
endless winter

check
engine light...
i call its bluff

leaving port
in a storm...the
not so swift family robinson

dough stuck
to the ceiling...the pizza man
throws up his hands

artic blast...
not as fun
as it sounds

rainy day
mother in law visit...
cold enough to snow

italian mother in law...
i tell her how good
my sauce is

30 years
after divorce...
i got to keep my hair

ground hogs day...
beyond a shadow of a doubt
10 more weeks of winter

mid winter night sky...
so clear and cold even
the stars come out to see

her name across
my forearm...still
under my skin

entering a new year...
all my bad habits
decide to come with me

greenwich village...
karaoke night
at the ymca

wedding night...
she calls him honey
he promises the moon

october hayride...
the hemp farmers wife offers
freshly baked brownies

finally...my team
comes to life and goes
to sudden death

taken
from henhouse...
poached eggs

slow news day...
this just in
...my cat

o negative...
a mosquito
orders it rare

neighborhood watch...
a hubcap
propped against a tree

learning to fly...
both the ant
and my sandwich

3 rain storms later...
the free couch at the curb
still free

hands this far apart...
the fishermen tells the story
of a missed putt

slowing down time...
i lean in to smell the
lilacs that are gone

street stickball rules...
one time out
per car

antique portrait...
color and smiling
yet to be invented

hermit crab
and recluse spider...
i give it a week

rewarding splendor
of a northern night sky...
constellation prizes

witness to a crime...
a chipmunk with a mouthful
wouldnt say bleep

stray cat under moonlight...
pauses looks up and moves on
...no regrets

red hens on the town...
girls night out ladies choice
free range chickens

alexa...
paint
my house

whenever feeling
shaken or stirred...
a dry martini

someone stole my heart...
ok i left it unlocked
...with the keys in it

divorce...
i brought you a poem
but it broke

mice...we often cross paths
living harmoniously
...i do the shopping

hospitality league
softball final score...
super 8 motel 6

spilled soda
on my laptop...
opening a tab

sunshine melting life
into waking bulbs...
a seed catalog

bent over the wheel
the plumber rolls down his widow
...just a crack

50 th class
reunion...former athletes
being wheeled in

Printed in Great Britain
by Amazon

83745429R00031